FOR our sons and daughter sorry because you see your mom at the phone as crazy talking with people was ignored us.

FOR God because we felt his presence every year without faith we may never can finish these hell
 we fight as David did with Goliath

For all those thanksgivings,Christmas,mother and father day we was alone and our family was separate was the hell in Earth be without our children.

For our cancer make us forget our fights every year with lender,title and assessor office

Because we never give up

these book is the ups and downs we been experience in our road & quest to save our home and i be learning all the banks suppose to have a report of the houses they have for sale well during our 23 years living and fighting for our home we found out is not true , banks keep their own agendas and make work and money "under sheets' nobody has laws but banks has profits. and the worst part is HOMEOWNER BILL RIGHTS nobody as a homeowners knows, people start to said

"homeowners are in those problems because they dont paid at time"

well going to be honest the answer is NOT ALWAYS IS THE REASON

few banks have people can not read, do grammar, learn, check or pe specific names of the homeowners where they really lived if is a COUNTY or PARISH of the geography of the State where the home is located ...is like have a real estate license come from a cracker jack candy popcorn .

we been see people in foreclosure as soldiers come back from wars, teachers 24 /7 working hard and paid their bills and 80% seniors and ill citizens.

they even have title companies come to work in different States without license to do so and many of them believe is like "wild, wild West" to do their own opinions and "clerical mistakes" USA   having problems the different way and each State have a trouble to do their own budgets but nobody really take a consideration what really happens, drugs , education , illness and many trouble even get involved in wars sometimes we don't have nothing to do .

Title companies add names for one home to another one even if the homeowners never have the idea what the are into, great news is check your credit report as us we became parents of older people almost our age + our own 3 teens. why? because the negligence of the Title company add us with that home as was ours and was recorder as ours under Sacramento Recorders office for almost 3 years, and we call almost every day emails, faxes, phones calls and was a nice customers services few times others racist remarks if we believe everything was free in USA.

But these new type of "profits: few assessors offices done under the law nobody realize affect everyone and everywhere these is done, clerical mistakes for names are so easy to make a mistakes as Smith for Smith or Garza for Garcia.

having a group of house or "pools" make a solution as the past the biggest Gangs can make for earn money with programs can suppose to help and give health the economy .Instead of that these type of identity theft is the same as selling drugs in the streets but is more refined situation if people dont have idea how these games are.

Many banks used the name of one family to qualify a group of 15 or 20 others and later on that family have extra cars, houses even children in their profiles even new credit cards from stores as Kohl's, Sears or even grocery type stores as well credit cards, with few companies don't believe or don't want to believe or their even agree to do the same and add that family as the member of the other 15 or 20 families even if their are not even know each other.

banks are easy to have attorneys tried to "bite" or even used words " you bark as dog" as one of the favorite phrases or even few title companies attorneys when suppose to explain their mistake their are as small 2 years old or making noises in the phone as their losing sign and make noises with their fingers and their mouths, the sad thing is these attorneys are students from Harvard or those very famous schools instead of teach them law as suppose to be teach them how to kill the law.

is many ways the banks let you or tried to scare you to give up your keys and walk out your home as far as we learn is new laws many of them are simple and easy to follow but the most important of them is continue to talk with your banks even if the hang up the phone to you or used a 2 year old wannabe attorney in their phones and make noises or tried to send you an apology letter for the low type of education Harvard or any of Law school give to them.

going to be days threats are the #1 way to scare you or even send people to take pictures to your home because for them follow the law is nothing write down in their education, many of them even assessors officers tried to said is a limited of time in your claim against them in case of identity theft go to your nearest police station and make a report the police officer going to give you a report # and keep for your records identity theft has not statute of limitation in all in all 50 State of US.,don't let them to urge you to used another attorney because is the law game" we ignored you because you going to get boring about it"

call them and do a claim if the county of assessor don't listen you everyone has a right and one of them is a file of document for their mistake going to denied their mistake continue to call and express your words in good manner. Teach them to said thanks and you're welcome many of them forgot that after their work with places as assessors offices, title companies and banks.

as a homeowners we have rights many of them protect us learn goggle the information and check what you can do.

never give up is the worst mistake a homeowner can do tried always you account be with FHA/HUD never do balloon type is the worst type of loan.

read, google and search

http://www.justice.gov/

many websites are in different languages and that is not one of the obstacles

your are the only one can bring justice to yourself

every State has their own representative with the Department of Justice google and search yours

California is

http://www.justice.gov/usao/biographies/duffy.html

as well each State has their own attorneys generals and for California we have 4

http://www.justice.gov/usao/districts/cae.html

in May 2011 the attorney general; in California created a the California Mortgage Fraud Strike force the strike force is made up of Department of Justice prosecutors and investigators charged with protection homeowners and bringing to justice those who would defraud them. it included three complementary teams a consumer enforcement team, a criminal enforcement team and a corporate fraud team, work together across the State
sometimes you believe these doesn't exist but it does is time a very good patient for you to look and tried to contact and express your own trouble, many counselors at HOPE are not working as suppose to be happens to us she was with me for more of 3 hours in the phone and we ending said " walk out from your home" as explain in my first book we found NACA is been change is new people working in these association and some of them are good and positive most of them nope, but was a great help for us and be honest with you we learn how to save our home and help us to save our home once and learn to save our home the second time.

in California the office of Kamala D Harris help you with letters never by phone but is a great tool in any homeowner tried to save their home

In addition the attorney general sponsored the California Homeowner BIll of rights which took effect on January 1 , 2013 the Homeowners BIll of rights protect the homeowners from dual tracking by forbidding a mortgage servicer from recording a notice of default or a notice of sale if a borrower has submitted a complete loan modification application or is in compliance with an approved loan modification.

if you think the homeowner bill of rights is being violated by your mortgage servicer we encourage you to submit a complaint to this office[attorney general}

https://oag.ca.gov/hbor

always seek help form the government first
 never agree to paid nobody in advance because that is fraud

http://portal.hud.gov/hudportal/HUD

as i tried to express our own experience in our own home companies are not 100% honest all the banks do money from documentation can be complete and honest and include few documents are not, clerical mistakes never suppose to happens and is always done, check your credit report every month it is possible

https://www.creditkarma.com/

check your credit can help you know how can be possible to found a job or buy a car or any other necessity

never give up we did more of 1000 phone calls to Louisiana from California since 2011, 2012 and 2013 never did nothing the change of the clerical mistake done to us was always for next day become a month after that become a year and never was the fix time of that clerical mistake in all.
we was in "hot oil" if i can said with everyone as IRS, DMV, and many others with extra cars and even extra children.

write letters as we did not matter few of most of them be ignored
"Dear Loan Workout Department
My husband and I currently cancer survivors and in treatment for cancer .We are requesting a review for our loan modification because we were faced with financial hardship because of a mistake made by our title company TITLE PLUS as well as GMFS. Due to this correctable clerical error that that went uncorrected for almost three years , my husband and i had our medical and disability benefits reduced , my job search was delayed and i had to delay cancer treatment because we could no longer afford to pay daily expenses like our mortgage for several months.
Sacramento home incorrectly put under our names and GMFS failure to correct mistake, starring November 28, 2011 we receive notifications from Sacramento County Assessor's office about a property
the that was under my name that was behind in taxes and utilities payments , we informed Sacramento Assessor that we only owed one home in Kern County. Shafter California , we had never owned a home in Sacramento , they did not believe us and required that we pay the back taxes and utilities immediately.
When i learned of this mistake i contacted robin Hogan at GMFS several times during 2012 with

numerous faxes and telephones calls even emails asking her to fix these problem, the problem never was fixed, therefore in 2012 and 2013 again i receive the package from the assessor's office at Sacramento to pay for those taxes and utilities on the Sacramento property , neither my husband or myself signed any affidavit , the fact that our names were on title was a clerical error or more likely identity theft.

I continued to contact GMFS regarding this mistake and they then referred me to Robin Campbell a GMFS attorney , i spoke with people at Title pLus who refused to fix these error the identity theft/unfixed error destroy my credit , my access to healthcare, my career as a result of these identity theft and failure to fix the error i was investigated by the internal revenue service (IRS) Social Security Administration {SSA} Medical,Medicare and Disability benefits agencies . They believe i was misrepresenting my property holdings on my benefits application by not telling them about additional property in Sacramento. Since i did not own the property in Sacramento or have anything to do with the property in question , my benefits were suspended unfairly and to my detriment. the reduction in my health and disability benefits led to a delay in my cancer treatment kept me from paying my own mortgage as well as delayed the cancer treatments of my husband,

FURthermore as i am a trained pharmacist technician my license to practice was put on hold for several months because the board of Pharmacy also found out the 2 address under my profile one in Shafter and one incorrected address at Sacramento Ca . Therefore my ability to find an additional job to supplement income to pay for the mortgage was thawerted again by the identity theft /uncorrected clerical error.As of the end of last year my name was finally removed from the property in Sacramento that should never have been there in the first place. i have an identity theft case open with the Shafter Police Department and i am finally getting my life in order. My benefits restored , I am receiving the treatment for my cancer and my next surgery coming March 19 2014, and {after that] i am also going on interviews to pursue the career I had to put on hold.I ask that your approve my loan modification/loan workout settlement , help me kept my home and move on from the nightmare of the last 2 years"

be specific with the problem go with the facts and tried all the time to have different way of communication as fax, email, phone # even if you can cellphone #, keep all your emails with the communication between you and your bank, ask questions because if happens as to us we have a great opportunity to check and show all the information since the date [in our case 2011] to when everything start to be a trouble.

i read a quote over facebook is complete true

"the news is not about news anymore, is about protecting some people destroying others and shoving a socialist agenda down the collective throats of America"
by Charlie Daniels

and i can said i agree with him because if you walk out from your home and let all these negligence go away or "clerical mistake "be fixed until the banks and title companies decide to do..

you lost all

is tedious? yes is sick? yes but is the way has to be when the pioneers came to America they dont found cellphones or computers ready for them, everything was suppose to be by hand and most of the time even lives was lost.
in these case we don't have to lost lives or houses we have laws was made for homeowners protections and is around us learn and used them.

you also going to found people tried to convince you to let it go and dont fight but as we learn is the most coward way to be ask them if they were in you place what they can do 88 % going to hang up the phone to you, because these people work only for a paycheck and they forgot the meaning of their job and how to do it.

we learn it with the Assessor office in another country different of us we call them for more of 800 days not move, not fixed the situation, ignored the facts and in the top of that used racist remarks
the easy way for many of these new"supervisors" to do their jobs.
these is an example of many hundreds of emails we did with the person who start our loan of course when these start was so educated it answers and sometimes very amicable later ..well you going to see

"we contact with GMFS about the mistake was fixed and never happens why?

to me

Please see the attached emails below. On 11/28/11 I emailed the title company and was told they had handled the problem.

I emailed them again today and ask them to check on it again, obviously it was not handled correctly in 11/11.

I will let you know when I hear back from them. I work for the mortgage company not the title company. The title company is responsible for filing the documents.

I will forward any information I get from them to you ASAP!

Thank you

Robin Hogan ǀ **Mortgage Consultant** ǀ **GMFS LLC**

7389 Florida Blvd Suite 200A ǀ Baton Rouge, LA ǀ 70806

Office: 225. 214.5062 ǀ Fax: 888.558.3193

of course these never happens and always or most of the time was the same answer
well these was as a ping pong ball nobody's fault but everyone knows these "clerical mistake"
was done and never fixed, in few words for these title companies is easy to used address from
different people and used them as mail addresses and for them these is a small mistake
as if you know everything comes in your credit, career and life

mistakes start to increase in different ways but was always an answer for us to be make us felt
safe [now we recognized we did the same mistake of millions of homeowners does, trust in you
lender}
these is one more example of that

From: Maria Garza [mailto:mariagarzasea@gmail.com]
Sent: Monday, August 22, 2011 8:54 PM
To: Hogan, Robin
Subject: Re: Documentation needed

These is mine?

Maria Garza

2011/8/22 Hogan, Robert Hogan@gmfslending.com>
Hi Martha, I have attached a Residential loan application for Andres to sign. This is from the last set of
documents I sent out, I got yours back but never got Andres signed doc back. We will need it in the file
when the file goes to closing. If you have returned this I apologize I cannot put my hands on it right now. So
please resend. Thanks Robin

Robin Hogan ǀ **Mortgage Consultant** ǀ **GMFS LLC**

7389 Florida Blvd Suite 200A ǀ Baton Rouge, LA ǀ 70806

Office: 225. 214.5062 ǀ Fax: 888.558.3193

Email : rhogan@gmfslending.com

NMLS# 351767

VISIT MY WEB PAGE

our names was not Martha or Andres problem with these banks are very systematic and classify
you as you race is, hispanic, white, african american, asian, hindu or any race you name be for

them and add you in a "pool of houses" and the nightmare starts because in those pools of houses everything get mixed, careers, credit cards, children, cars , even taxes.

these was the problem of the "pool houses" a family in different county default their home and we receive the notices why? simple our names was in the recorder assessor office of the county that home was situated and these email arrive to me...heads up nobody listen to us and nobody looks for fix the mistake since 2011, 2012, 2013 we was also the homeowners of the same property.. one thing is we are hispanic roots another one is if we know everyone in USA as us? nope

but these is the start of the mistake cost us my medical insurance, career and almost our home:

Hi Andrea and Teri,

Ms. Garza called me today and said she got a phone call from Sacramento County (where the Valles' home is) stating that she is on title with the Valles and part owner of the property with them. Can you make sure there was not some type of mix up on the title for the Valley's loan?

I have attached the HUD's for your reference. Thanks!

Robin Hogan ı **Mortgage Consultant** ı **GMFS LLC**

7389 Florida Blvd Suite 200A | Baton Rouge, LA | 70806

Office: 225. 214.5062 ı Fax: 888.558.3193

Email : rhogan@gmfslending.com

NMLS# 351767

VISIT MY WEB PAGE

Maria Garza maria garza   10/3/13
sea@gmail.com

to administrator

these email was sent since 2011 and the situation instead to get better was worst

more letters from Sacramento ask us for taxes and utilities from a home we never own and more and more trouble in my medical benefits and even my own career.

since 2011 GMFS AND TITLE PLUS ADD OUR NAME TO A HOME LOCATED
AT SACRAMENTO

1

A letter of apology is not going to cover all the mess we are now

we spent more of $24,000 sending documentation and nobody listen to us we
have to call

Hogan, Robert Hogan@gmfslending.com>

to me

Please see the attached emails below. On 11/28/11 I emailed the title company and was told
they had handled the problem.

I emailed them again today and ask them to check on it again, obviously it was not handled
correctly in 11/11.

I will let you know when I hear back from them. I work for the mortgage company not the title
company. The title company is responsible for filing the documents.

I will forward any information I get from them to you ASAP!

Thank you

Robin Hogan ∣ **Mortgage Consultant** ∣ **GMFS LLC**

Hi Andrea,

Can you please check and see what happened with this? The Garza's in Shafter have gotten foreclosure
notices for the Valles' home in Sacramento. This was supposed to be addressed in November and now Mrs.
Garza is calling me ranting and raving because she is certain that this will ruin her credit! I tried to call
Malinda Valles but had to leave a message. Mrs. Garza stated she has received 8 seizure notices from
Sacramento regarding the Valles' property.

Teri told me at that time that there was a mix up and she was checking into it.

Please try to find out if this address correction was made and it the Valles' have been receiving their tax notices and I think we should check on the escrow as well and make sure it is applied correctly.

Thanks Robin

not title company, not lender, not servicer fix these negligence in all nobody want to listen to us and just let go, add us in different trouble for them was business as usual for us was a nightmare.

is the time as a homeowner to think the situation can be positive or not and as well if you need an attorney, basically we learn even attorneys make mistakes and later on tried to justify them and in that moment is when you need to read all your documents more of 3 times and check if your answers are complete or not.

learn to ask questions, check all the points you can figure out and points you can not GOOGLE or used BING and research believe me is a great tool have the complete information over all and for once with you.

even the assessor's office in each county of California suppose to have rules and regulations and many of them suppose be under the law but as we learn letters by fax and money be enough for few assessor officers to record a document even if people never is present in all be signed and stamped and even if that family call them ignored them and let see if the phone calls stop and these officers forgot about what job they do.

title plus make for us few letters with their explanation about their mistakes for them is "sorry apologize and forget about it"

by law is negligence, identity theft.

August 9, 2013

CERTIFIED RETURN RECEIPT NO.
7006 2760 0002 5972 2052

Mr. and Mrs. Ramon Garza
857 Clarence Street
Shafter, California 93263

RE: Our file no. A-20110708181

Dear Mr. and Mrs. Garza:

As you know a Grant Deed was created by our office for Ray and Malinda Valles' property. As you can see from the top left of the attached original Grant Deed, it incorrectly specified for tax notices to be sent to you, Ramon D. Garza and Maria P. Garza, at your home at 857 Clarence Street, Shafter, California.

The Valles' have defaulted on their home loan and unfortunately the foreclosing law firm used the tax notice address on the Grant Deed as one of the places to send notices of default, care of you. This resulted in you receiving a copy of the Valles' notices of default but in no way did those notices implicate you as being in default on any loan.

Upon learning of the error, TitlePlus took steps to correct the Deed. A Corrective Grant Deed was prepared correcting the tax notice information by removing your information and inputting the Valles' information. The Corrective Grant Deed was recorded and I have attached a copy of the Deed showing the correction to the tax notice section and reflecting recording information as indicated by the Sacramento County Recorder. The recording information verifies that the Sacramento County Recorder has received the Corrective Grant Deed and it is now public record.

The foreclosing law firm in the Valles matter has been provided a copy of the Corrective Grant Deed and has advised us they will no longer send the Valles' foreclosure correspondence to you or your address.

At this point there is no further action required on our part. We apologize for the aggravation this has caused you. However, since the corrective work is now complete, we respectfully request you discontinue contacting GMFS and TitlePlus. There is nothing either Company can further help you with at this time. Therefore, continuing to contact GMFS, TitlePlus and their representatives will not benefit you in any way.

Thank you for your attention to this matter.

Sincerely,

Jacques B. Favret, esq.

7369 Florida Blvd, Suite 200B, Baton Rouge, LA 70806
Phone: (225) 709-3500   Fax: (225) 709-3501

August 9, 2013

Mr. and Mrs. Ramon Garza CERTIFIED RETURN RECEIPT NO. 857 Clarence Street 7006 2760 0002 5972 2052 Shafter, California 93263

RE: Our file no. A-20110708181 Dear Mr. and Mrs. Garza:

As you know a Grant Deed was created by our office for Ray and Malinda Valles' property. As you can See from the top left of the attached original Grant Deed, it incorrectly specified for tax notices to be sent to you, Ramon D. Garza and lVlaria P. Garza, at your home at 857 Clarence Street, Shatter, California.

The Valles' have defaulted on their home loan and unfortunately the foreclosing law firm used the tax notice address on the Grant Deed as one of the places to send notices of default, care of you. This resulted in you receiving a copy of the Valles' notices of default but in no way did those notices implicate you as being in default on any loan.

Upon learning of the error, TitLe Pius took steps to correct the Deed. A Corrective Grant Deed was prepared correcting the tax notice information by removing your information and inputting the Valles' information. The Corrective Grant Deed was recorded and I have attached a copy of the Deed showing the correction to the tax notice section and reflecting recording information as indicated by the Sacramento County Recorder. The recording information verifiers that the Sacramento County Recorder has received the Corrective Grant Deed and it is now public record.

The foreclosing in 'the Valles matter has been provided a copy of the Corrective Grant Deed and has advised us they will no longer send the Valles' foreclosure correspondence to you or your address.

At this point there is no further action required on our part. We apologize for the aggravation this has caused you. However, since the corrective work is now complete, we respectfully request you discontinue contacting Gl VlFS and TitlePlus. There is nothing either Company can further help you with at this time. Therefore, continuing to contact GMFS, TitlePlus and their representatives will not benefit you in any way.

Thank you for your attention to this matter.

7389 Florida Blvd, Suite 2005, Baton Rouge, LA 70806 Phone: (225) 709-3500 Fax: (225) 709-3501

point is we contact with the LOuisiana authorities and

1.

The undersigned grantnrmdeclamß) want me documentary muster eax @um NAW CHANGE

TRANSFER and is

Chuck Tumblr 111267

FÜR A VALUABLE CDNSIDERATÍON, receipt of which Is hereby acknowledged, BAY VALLES, IU AND

VALLES

executed the Instrument. ,

and official seal.

Signatum

Exempt from transfer tax under cada 1.1925

Grantors and Grammes are comprised of the; samß'pàrtiaa and their proportional interest remains the same immediately following transfer.

BONA FIDE GUEST

Sacramento County Recorçier

Check Number 9027 l Friday, JUL 19, 2013 11:39:17 RM RECORDING REQUESTED BY Ttl Pd $30.00 Rept t# 0007879125

AND WHEN RECORDED MAIL ID NAME: Title Plus, LLC

ADDRESS: 7389 Florida Blvd, Ste ZOOB

CITY: Baton Rouge

STATES ZIPZ LA 70806

MAH. TAX STATEMENTS TO

NAME: Raymundo Valles, HI and Malìnda Valles ADDRESS: 8375 Country GLen Court

CITY: Sacramento

STATE Z|PI CA, 95828

Title Order No. Escrow or Loan No.: A20110207492 SPACE ABOVE THIS LINE FOR RECORDER'S USE

CORRECTIVE GRANT DEED

     FOR VALUABLE CONSIDERATION, receipt of which is hereby acknowledged, RAY VALLES, ill AND MALINDA VALLES, Herein Represented by Vince, Attorney in Fact by virtue of GMFS, L.L.C Correction Agreement Limited Power of Attorney, a copy of which is attached hereto and made a part hereof as 'Exhibit B', Does hereby GRANT to

RAYMUNDO VALLES, lll AND MALINDA VALLES

That certain real property in the City of Sacramento, County of Sacramento, State of California, described in Exhibit "A", attached hereto and incorporated herein by reference

This corrective Grand Deed is recorded for the sole purpose of correcting certain provisions (Noted Below) of that certain Grant Deed dated August 24, 2011, and recorded November 8, 2011, in Sacramento County Official Records in Book 20111108, Page 0525.

NOTE: This Corrective Grant Deed is being recorded to correct the erroneous information as to whom and where Tax Statements are mailed to nd the Title order No. Escrow or Loan No. as contained in the original Grant Deed. l/

STATE OF LOUISIANA PARISH OF EAST BATON ROUGE

On July 10, 2013, before me, the undersigned a Notary Public, personally appeared Kelì Vince personally known to me (or proved to me on the basis of satisfactory evidence) to be the persons Whose names are' subscribed to, the Within instrument and acknowledged to me that they executed the same in their authorized capacity ies), pursuant to that Limited Power of Attorney dated August 24, 2011 authorizing GMFS, LLC to correct clerical errors in the Deed, a copy which is attached hereto and made a part hereof, and that by their Signatures on the instrument the persons, or the entity upon behalf of which the persons acted, executed the instrument.

WITNESS my Tidy offííal seal. Signature L (Seal) JACQUES B. FAVRET ~ BAR ROLL NO* 19565

STATE OF LOUISIANA COMMISSION IS FOR LIFE

As well we found companies or "law firms" promise to help homeowners if you "visit them in their office" these is 50% -50% going to listen to you or for them to know what "news" around the Real Estate community is around and don't do nothing

many of them make commercials with "real cases" and all is pre- done or lie

so before you do or travel to these offices ask to check your papers first before travel and give them "heads up" and you come out without "good news"

these companies speak with you very nice by phone , give incorrect information in their websites and you have to "look" for the correct number.

keep near you or a least same county you live.

yes !!!! you going to found companies promise to help you and after you done and explain them your situation can said "move out your home"

is critical for you to be strong for all these type of "laws attorneys" can be 2 faces one of them promise you help and other take a cup of wine with your own bank attorney.

it is heavy and harsh time for each family member , but hang in there is really good places can help you.

EXHIBIT A

SITUATED IN THE COUNTY OF SACRAMENT, STATE OF CALIFORNIA:

LOT 71, AS SHOWN ON THE "PLAT OF SOUTHFIELD" RECORDED IN BOOK 170 OF MAPS, MAP NO. 10, RECORDS OF SAID COUNTY.

TAX ID NO: 115-0700-088-000

BEING THE SAME PROPERTY CONVEYED BY GRANT DEED:

GRANTOR: YVONNE J. FLORENDO, A MARRIED WOMAN, AS HER SOLE AND SEPARATE PROPERTY, AS TO AN UNDIVIDED 1/3 INTEREST AND GLORIA A. FLORENDO, AN UNMARRIED WOMAN, WHO ACQUIRED TITLE INCORRECTLY AS A MARRIED WOMAN, AS TO AN UNDIVIDED 1/3 INTEREST AND MARIA F. SLACK, A MARRIED WOMAN, A/K/A/ MARIA SLACK, AS HER SOLE AND SEPARATE PROPERTY, AS TO AN UNDIVIDED 1/3 INTEREST.

GRANTEE: RAY VALLES III AND MALINDA VALLES, HUSBAND AND WIFE, AS JOINT TENANTS

DATED: 11/30/2000

RECORDED: 12/22/2000

DOC#/BOOK-PAGE: 20012221655

ADDRESS: 8375 COUNTRY GLEN COURT, SACRAMENTO, CA 95828

END OF SCHEDULE A

EXHIBIT A SITUATED IN THE COUNTY OF SACRAMENTO, STATE OF CALIFORNIA:

LOT 71, AS SHOWN ON THE PLAT OF SOUTHFIELD" RECORDED iN BOOK 17D OF MAPS, MAP NO.10, RECORDS OF SAID COUNTY.

TAX ID NO 115~O700-088-OOO BEING THE SAME PROPER"l CONVEYED BY GRANT DEEDI

GRANTOR: YVONNE .I. FLORENDO, A MARRIED WOMAN, AS HER SOLE AND SEPARATE PROPERTY, AS TO AN UNDIVIDED 1/3 INTEREST AND GLORIA A. FLORENDO, AN UNMARRIED WOMAN, WHO ACQUIRED TITLE INCORRECTLY AS A MARRIED WOMAN, AS TO AN UNDIVIDED 1/3 INTEREST AND MARIA F. SLACK, A MARRIED WOMAN, A/K/A/ MARIA SLACK, AS HER SOLE AND SEPARATE PROPERTY, AS TO AN UNDIVIDED 1/3 INTEREST.

GRANTEE RAY VALLES Hl AND MALINDA VALLES, HUSBAND AND WIFE, AS JOINT TENANTS DATED: ll/BO/ZDDO

RECORDED 112/22/ZOOO

DOC#/BOOK~PAG E12001222~1655

ADDRESSI 8375 COUNTRY GLEN COURT, SACRAMENTO, CA 95828

END OF SCHEDULE A

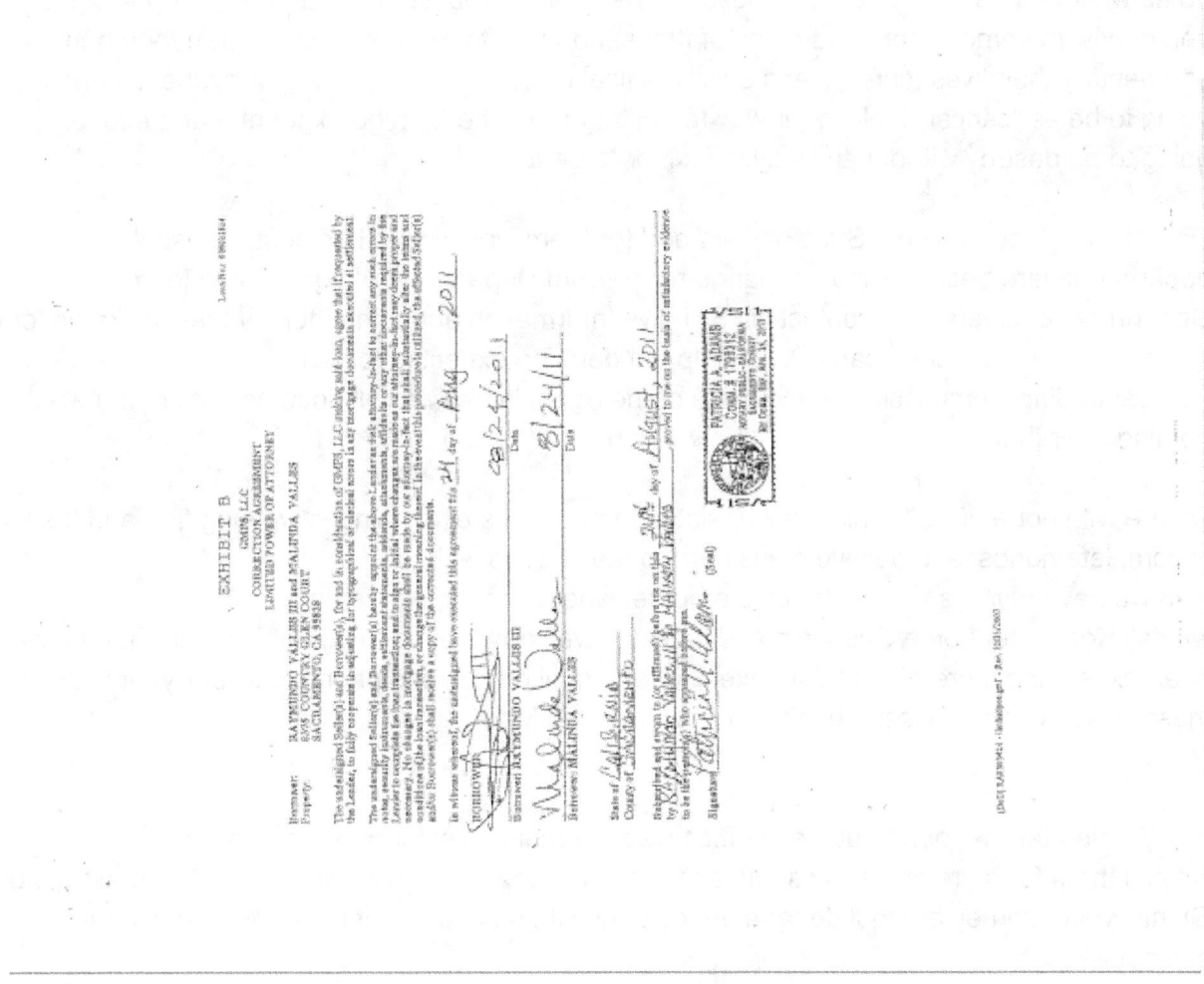

GMFS, LLC CORRECTION AGREEMENT » LIMiteD POWER OF ATTORNEY

RAYMUNDO VALLES III und MALINDA VALLES 8375 COUNTRY GLEN COURT SACRAMENTO, CA 95828

Borrower:

Property:

The undersized Seller@ and Borrower(s), for and ln ismeretlen of GMFS, LLC malling seldloßn, agree that llrequesturl by the Lender, te [elly cooperate In adjusting for typographical or clerical errors In any moñgage documents executed at settlement.

The unders and Sellem) and Borrower(s) hereby appoint the above Lender as their attorney~in fact to correct any such errors ln . notes, seourñy Instruments, deeds, settlement statements, addenda, attachments, affidavlte or any other documents required by the Lender to complete the loan tension; and to sign or' initial where changes are made as our ettemeyer-infect pny deem proper and necessary. Ranges in mortgage documents sweii be made by our attomey-ln-'feet that snail substantially alter the terms and conditions of the loan transaction, or change lite general meaning thereof. In the event this procedure is utilized, the affected Seiler@ and/orBol'l'ower(e) shell receive a copy of the corrected documents.

the point with these documents is we never live ,reside or buy a home in Sacramento and we contact with the consolidated and recorder officers for more of 2 years and half 2011, 2012 and 2013 instead of listen and look for the trouble the same mistake was in our names add in other home without an affidavit from us these shows how the real state companies are playing rude and dirty with homeowners and many of thousand ways to remove families from their homes and destroy their lives ,careers and even medical insurance because as far as these continue going to be as "cancer" looking for way to destroy the base for a good country and economy going to be destroy without any way to fix it or "tape it"

we been contact with Real State officers and for them was simple business as usual, departments are been closing or change name from Department of corporation for the Department of Oversight...contact wit FBI give information about the identity theft is like as for a miracle be done because can ask for help but don't be expected for help.
Federal trading Commission is one more of the agencies as well fill documentation and was nothing after that.

we are with hope of California legal Assistance and looks everything is working fine and the way is complete honest and believe me is hard to feel that as well
also we have FHA [safe way to have a homeowner mortgage payment}
we call Keep your home California and looks as well good place to go but if we are honest we been expending more of $9000 in faxes, letters, mail,copies and phone calls per year with all these "places and servicers, banks and even Ginnie Mae"

yes Ginnie Mae we found out these office was the main investor of our home
we call them for more of 40 times and as far as i know 2011, 2012, 2013 and 2014 nobody from Ginnie Mae attorney or legal department contact with us in all, so if these office exist never contact with us in all.

our point to do these books is for give information if we can do everyone can do as well and nobody has the right to said you can not do it in all
not expect tv stations help you because their "ratings" can be in trouble
point is maybe later help us with add these mess in the media as well.

as a homeowners need to be more reachable to learn and know their rights, look over the internet call your representative people [Senators, district officers, assessor offices.etc] and check the internet
google the information or bing and believe me you can found the way to fix these trouble for yourselves.

as a community help others to learn how to save their homes and teach them how you learn to do yourself i do..we talk with people and we tried to help.

banks or servicers promise to help you never happens
as happens to us

these is one more example

Hello,
Good Morning Mrs. Garza,

RE: Loan Number
Property Address:
                    SHAFTER CA 93263

Thank you for providing us with this information as per our phone conversation today. First, we would like to apologize for the delay, inconvenience and frustration you are experiencing. The information you have provided with immediately be submitted for review as a "High Urgency" matter.

You will be contacted to make sure that your issue is handled accordingly.

Again, we apologize for the inconvenience you have experienced.

Sincerely,

Seldi Kr

Many others even blame us for these clerical mistake and name me dog or said "Mrs Garza you barking as a dog"
maybe is the way i talk but is our right destroy ? yes and these people don't have the right to let it go… and they did since 2011 to 2014….

you can make a "friendship" with realtor who do you mortgage payments but you have to be careful that "friendship" is no replace later for a full pool of lies as our adventures

8/18/11

Maria Garza <maria garza sea@gmail.com>

to Robin

ith the payment of $580? but where I send to Louisiana in the same address in your business card?
wow that was a new for usks

Mary
ps we start our payments until October? and the small loan of $1047

2011/8/18 Hogan, Robert Hogan@gmfslending.com>

Hogan, Robert Hogan@gmfslending.com>

to me

Yes the money order you will give the notary at the closing will cover your October payment, so if you have not received any information by the middle of October you will need to mail your November payment to GMFS at the address on my card.

Robin Hogan ׀ **Mortgage Consultant** ׀ **GMFS LLC**

7389 Florida Blvd Suite 200A ׀ Baton Rouge, LA ׀ 70806

Office: 225. 214.5062 ׀ Fax: 888.558.3193

Email : rhogan@gmfslending.com

NMLS# 351767

but later these can be the only good memory you going to have from these great opportunity to qualify in a program suppose to promise to help homeowners save their homes but with the risk of negligence , identity theft and ignorance damage your lives and careers forever.
our point is if the banks does mistakes the homeowners need to live with them forever because for them mistakes make for the companies their hire are not their problem in all
so the title company can make a mistake o r clerical error and is good
the assessor office can make clerical mistakes to don't check or research the title companies if they have license to work in California or not and that is not liability in all

and the homeowners are the only guilty ones in these clerical mistakes or identity theft

these is an example happens to us

Mrs. Garza, considering the tone of all of the written correspondence and numerous phone calls that you have made to GMFS LLC representatives, it is apparent that you are of the opinion that GMFS LLC has "wronged" you in some way. From the inception of your loan transaction with GMFS LLC, they have gone above and beyond to assist you. At the time of origination of your loan, the total due on your mortgage was over $200,000. You took advantage of the opportunity that GMFS LLC gave you to participate in the Hope for Homeowner's Loan. Apparently, at the time you refinanced with GMFS LLC, you owed more on your home than the property was worth. GMFS LLC provided you with the opportunity to write your loan down to a little over $60,000. In essence, a debt of over $140,000 was forgiven to help you save your home. Clearly you can see that this was a great opportunity for you and your husband to try to get back on your feet.

Once your loan closed with Title Plus, it is apparent that an error was made by TitlePlus that caused a bit of confusion. When you became aware of the error, you contacted Ms. Robin Hogan. Robin Hogan, who worked for GMFS LLC at that time, tried to facilitate communication between you and TitlePlus as TitlePlus tried to correct the error. Hence, once again, a representative from GMFS LLC tried to help you. At all times throughout your refinance experience, GMFS LLC tried to help you, yet you continue to show frustration towards GMFS LLC even though another company, TitlePlus, made the error.

On August 9, 2013, a letter was sent to you from TitlePlus via certified mail. The letter explained that an error was made, it was
corrected and you were provided with copies of the Corrective Deed. TitlePlus apologized for the aggravation that the error caused you, and explained that since the corrective work was completed, there was no further action required on their part. TitlePlus also asked that you discontinue contacting them and GMFS LLC; however, you have not complied with that request. You have now said that you will be withholding your mortgage payment because you expect TitlePlus and GMFS LLC to pay for "these months."

I would like to remind you that the Promissory Note that you signed at the closing obligates you to make your mortgage payment until the loan is satisfied. If you breach the contract that you signed, by not paying your mortgage payment, GMFS LLC will seek all remedies in law and equity to protect its interest. **GMFS LLC will not make any of your mortgage payments.**

GMFS LLC respectfully requests that you discontinue contacting this company regarding the issues that you seem to have with the error that was made by TitlePlus. You are to cease all communication with Ms. Robin Hogan. She is no longer an employee of GMFS LLC. I expect you to comply with this request, and if you do not, GMFS LLC reserves the right to pursue all remedies in law and equity to motivate you to cease all communication with this company regarding the error that was made by TitlePlus.

Please be reminded that you need to make your mortgage payments, and I appreciate your attention to this matter.

Sincerely,

xxxxxxx

****
****

so what to do ? continue to call them and show them their mistakes are destroying your lives and even the treats or words they used against you communication need to be open always

these is one more of the example;

April 4, 2014

Mr. & Mrs. Ramon Garza
857 Clarence Street
Shafter, California 93263

Re: State of California – Business, Consumer Services and Housing Agency
       Complaint – 5603
       Maria Garza

Dear Mr. & Mrs. Garza
 In response to your most recent complaint against GMFS LLC, I would like to reiterate that this company has gone above and beyond to assist you from the inception of your loan transaction. GMFS LLC provided you with the opportunity, via the Hope for Homeowner's Loan program, to write down over $60,000 on your mortgage; in essence, a debt of over $140,000 was forgiven to help save your home. Recently, within the last few months, once again, GMFS LLC participated in a conference call with you, our sub-servicing partners and the Louisiana Attorney General's office to help you come up with a resolution to save your home from foreclosure due to default in your mortgage payments.   During that conference call, you were specifically told about what was needed from you in order to go through the Loss Mitigation qualifying stage.

We explained that you needed to provide "all" items requested by a specific deadline, including the monetary amount, to begin the Loss Mitigation process. You said that you understood what was required and understood that there was a deadline, AND you agreed to the terms, yet you never supplied the monetary amount that was requested.

At this point, GMFS LLC has done all that can possibly be done to try to assist you. Attached, please find my letter to you dated September 9, 2013 where I reminded you about the Promissory Note that you signed at the closing which contractually binds you to make your mortgage payments. Since you decided to stop making your payments AND failed to provide all items required to begin the Loss Mitigation program, GMFS LLC reserves the right to seek all remedies in law and equity to protect its interest.

Sincerely,

XXXXXXXXXXXX

XXXXXXXXXXXXXXXXXXXXXXXXXXXXXXXXXXXXXXXXXXXXXXXXXXXXXXXXXXXXXXXXXXXXXXXXXXXXXXXXXXXXXXXXXXXXXXXXXX
XXXXXXXXXXXXXXXXXXXXXXXXXXXXXXXXXXXXXXXXXXXXXXXXXXXXXXXXXXXXXXXXXXXXXXXXXXXXXXXXXXXXXXXXXXXXXXXXXX

as always treats going to be treats arriving to your emails and phone calls because for them clerical mistakes need to be a blessings for them is "a great job to help you"

one of the things you have to be sure is laws in each State as Federal Level as well and that can help the homeowners and the renters [in case you rent a home as well} used the internet, google it or bing and read all about laws is necessary to be at time of each new law and how to protect you

California has a brief guide i copy and paste here and why i do that because we know how hard is to fix a clerical mistakes or negligence banks and title companies can do to homeowners

each State has different program please be aware of all of them..

LOAN DEFAULT AND FORECLOSURE:
A BRIEF GUIDE FOR CALIFORNIA HOMEOWNERS

Compiled by:		Provided by:
UNIVERSITY OF SAN FRANCISCO,		COMMUNITY LEGAL SERVICES IN E. PALO ALTO
SCHOOL OF LAW		2117 (B) UNIVERSITY AVENUE
PREDATORY LENDING CLINIC		EAST PALO ALTO, CA 94303
		TEL: (650) 326-6440

With the generous assistance of Fenwick and West, LLC.

February, 2009

LOAN DEFAULT AND FORECLOSURE:
A BRIEF GUIDE FOR CALIFORNIA HOMEOWNERS

This guide is designed to help homeowners understand the options available to them in foreclosure. It describes the foreclosure process, the documents homeowners may expect to receive in foreclosure and highlights some of the important options and considerations homeowners must be aware of when their home is threatened by foreclosure.

Actions You Can Take to Save Your Home
If You Are Behind or Not Able to Pay Your Mortgage

It is important to know that your mortgage company would always prefer to keep you in your home rather than foreclose. They are in the business of providing mortgages, not owning or selling homes.

It is in your best interests to talk to a counselor, a lawyer, or contact your mortgage company directly so you can keep your home.

Talk to a housing counselor.

Look for a **HUD certified counselor.** The Department of Housing and Urban Development has trained and certified loan counselors who will assist you **free of charge** and can negotiate with the mortgage company's representative or "servicer" on your behalf. Servicers are often permitted by the agreements governing loans to renegotiate your loan terms, a process known as "work-out" or "loss mitigation." This process may reduce your monthly payments, give you a few months without loan payments, delay payment of arrears or make it possible to otherwise change the payments on your home loan.

The Department of Housing and Urban Development's Web site, www.hud.gov/foreclosure, has a nationwide directory of counseling agencies, or you can call them at (800) 569-4287. **Services are free.** Advice is also available at the **Homeowner's Hope Hotline** at (888) 995-HOPE.

Contact a lawyer.

If you were misled or not fully informed by a broker or mortgage company about the terms of the loan, you might be able to "rescind" (cancel) the loan. You may also be entitled to damages. If you cannot afford a lawyer, call your local **Bar Association or Legal Aid** office and ask them to refer you to a lawyer.

Contact information for local **Legal Aid Societies** can be found at www.dca.ca.gov/publications/guide/legal_index.shtml.

Call your mortgage company.

Ask for the "loss-mitigation" or "work-out" department and try to modify the loan terms. Be smart about modifying your loan. Many properties are worth less than the mortgages they secure; is it in your best interests to keep a property that is worth less than your mortgage?   Be realistic about whether you can make the "modified" payments. Keep in mind that most modification documents contain a "waiver". That means when you sign the modification documents you give up any legal rights you may have and you give up the right to take your mortgage company to court. **Before you sign anything, take the papers to a lawyer or counselor to be sure you fully understand what you are signing.** It is a legal document and you will be bound by the terms in the modification agreement.

How Mortgages in California are Foreclosed

Foreclosures vary from state to state. The following information will help you to understand the California foreclosure process.

California is known as a Title Theory state where the mortgage company (i.e. bank) holds the title to the property while you live on the land and continue to make mortgage payments. The document that secures the title is usually called a "deed of trust" but may also be referred to as a mortgage. California has a complicated set of rules concerning foreclosures. The entire foreclosure process is described below.

How are mortgages in California foreclosed?

In general, foreclosure means that when you miss a payment or two, the bank sends an official notice that you are in the foreclosure process. Then you have a period of time to cure the deficiency. If you cannot do that, the mortgage company pursues foreclosure through either judicial or non-judicial means. An auction is then held and the property is sold to the highest bidder.

The primary method of foreclosure in California involves what is known as **non-judicial foreclosure**. This type of foreclosure does **not** involve court action. When the deed of trust/mortgage is initially signed, it will usually contain a provision called a power of sale clause. This allows the trustee (usually a title company) to sell the property to satisfy the defaulted loan. The trustee acts as a representative of the mortgage company to sell the property, which typically occurs in the form of an auction.

California has a requirement known as the one-action rule. If a foreclosure is completed by non-judicial means (outside of court), then the mortgage company cannot pursue a second action against you if the auction proceeds do not meet the amount due on the property.

If a foreclosure is **judicial**, the house may be sold and a separate judgment may be obtained against you for the remaining balance due on the loan (up to the full amount of the loan plus foreclosure costs) if the auction proceeds do not meet the balance due on the property.

Most loans are foreclosed using non-judicial foreclosure, but a mortgage company has the option of using judicial foreclosure. Since this process takes longer than non-judicial foreclosure, it is rarely used. In California non-judicial remedies have stringent notice requirements and the mortgage documents are required to contain the power of sale language in order to use this type of foreclosure method.

Key Points in the Foreclosure Process

Missing one or more mortgage payments means you are in default.

If you miss one or two payments, a mortgage company will usually contact you to demand payment and may offer to modify the loan. *This is a good time to consult a counselor or lawyer and ask them to negotiate with the mortgage company.*

Receiving a Notice of Default.

If you do nothing in response to the mortgage company's attempts to contact you, or you cannot come to an agreement with them, the mortgage company generally sends a further notice advising that they are declaring a "default" of the loan obligations. The official notice is called the **Notice of Default** and is filed with the

County Recorder's Office by the trustee (usually a title company). A copy must be mailed to you. The Notice of Default must spell out the specific breach of contract. If you want to know whether a Notice of Default has been filed against your property, consult with the County Recorder in the County where the property is located. All interested parties must be served and notified of the foreclosure.

The filing of the Notice of default begins the **Reinstatement Waiting Period**, which is **90 days**. This is the time period that you get to cure the debt by paying off all overdue payments (i.e. bringing the mortgage current).

Selling the property - Notice of Trustee's Sale.

After the 90 day Reinstatement Waiting Period is up, the Trustee has the obligation to do a final check to see if the deficiency has been cleared. After this check, a **Notice of Sale** of the property can be issued and you must be served with this notice. The

Notice of Sale must be published once per week for a period of at least 20 days. The Trustee is also obligated to post in a conspicuous place on the property and in at least one off-property place, a sign notifying the public of the upcoming sale. After the 20 day Publication Period is up, the auction for sale of the home can be held.

As stated earlier, the Trustee does not have to go to court to have the right to sell the property. The sale is an auction and the property is sold to the highest bidder. If anyone other than the beneficiary (mortgage company) purchases the property, they must have cash in hand.

The laws that govern California foreclosures are found in California Civil Code, Section 2924. To view these statutes on the Web, you can visit: http://www.leginfo.ca.gov.

If the property is foreclosed through the court system in a judicial foreclosure, there is a right of redemption period after foreclosure. However, foreclosures that are non-judicial have **no** period of redemption in California. Most foreclosures in California are non-judicial, so more often than not, **once the sale of the defaulted property is complete, the sale is final.**

California Foreclosure Timeline

Day 1-Day 90	Day 91-Day 110	Day 111 or more
Redemption Period	**Publication Period**	**Trustee's Sale**
Lasts 90 days from the recordation of the Notice	Lasts 20 days from the end of Redemption	Held 21 days after first publication

of Default		

After the property is sold at the Foreclosure Sale.

Whoever owns your home cannot just change the locks to the home. The new owner must serve you with a 3-day written notice to quit, and then must take you through the formal eviction process in order to get possession of the property. That process takes about 30-45 days.

If someone knocks on your door and tells you to get out, do not panic. No one has the right to simply tell you to leave without going through the formal eviction process. If you feel threatened or unsafe, do not answer your door, or call the police. The new owner must follow the formal legal process and evict you in order to have you leave.

Alternative Options to Foreclosure

Contact your existing mortgage company

As stated earlier, the first thing you may want to do is contact your existing mortgage company. Some mortgage companies are willing to work with those who have fallen behind on their payments and have defaulted on their loans.

Forbearance

Like a payment plan, forbearance is an agreement between you and the mortgage company that reinstates the delinquent loan through the payment of a lump sum or

a schedule of payments over a period of time. If you are behind on your payment by $2,000, for example, the mortgage company may allow you to pay the money back through installment payments over six months. The mortgage company may decide, on the other hand, to allow you to pay a reduced monthly payment until you have an opportunity to get back on your feet and pay any remaining arrearages in one lump sum. Generally, these agreements will not exceed more than 12 months, but before you sign anything, consult with a lawyer or counselor.

Deed in Lieu of Foreclosure

A deed in lieu of foreclosure is an alternative where you voluntarily give up the property title to the mortgage company. Generally, this is a last ditch effort to avoid the negative consequences of foreclosure. Here, you tell your mortgage company that they do not need to bother with the formalities of a foreclosure proceeding because you will simply turn over your title to the property rather than lose it. This is sometimes known as a "friendly foreclosure" because it is a mutual agreement between you and the mortgage company and is not forced upon you by use of the power of sale.

The advantage of the deed in lieu of foreclosure is that it lessens the damage to your credit history. Although it is not nearly as good as paying off the note on time, it is better than a foreclosure. The mortgage company will still report the surrender to credit rating agencies, which will significantly lower your credit rating, but you can point to the surrender to indicate to future lenders that you acted responsibly upon realizing that you would be obliged to default on your note.

Short Sale

When the mortgage company agrees to do a short sale in real estate, it means they are accepting less than the total amount due. Not all mortgage companies will accept short sales or discounted payoffs, especially if it would make more financial sense to foreclose; moreover, not all sellers nor all properties qualify for short sales. A short sale means your mortgage company is accepting a discounted payoff to release an existing mortgage. Just because a property is listed with short sale terms does not mean the mortgage company will accept your offer, even if you

accept it.

Be aware that you need not be in default -- to have stopped making mortgage payments -- before a mortgage company will consider a short sale. A mortgage company may consider a short sale if you are current on your payments, but the value on your home has fallen. You may have over-encumbered (owe more than the home is worth), so a discounted price might bring the price in line with market value, but will not bring the loan to a price below market value. A short sale negatively affects your credit, but it is not as bad as foreclosure.

Can a Bankruptcy Help Save My Home?

Talk to a lawyer or counselor about the benefits and drawbacks of filing for bankruptcy. Filing bankruptcy should be considered with great care. It stays on your record for up to 10 years and can have significant negative impact on your life for this duration.

The filing of bankruptcy triggers an automatic stay which stops all creditors from any action to collect their claim while the bankruptcy is pending. This will temporarily stop foreclosure in most cases. Nevertheless, a foreclosure may still continue in limited situations such as when multiple bankruptcy cases have been filed in a row or if the property was transferred to your name immediately prior to filing.

The biggest mistake that people make is waiting until a few days prior to the foreclosure sale date to look into bankruptcy as an option. The best time to consult with a bankruptcy attorney is either before or early on during the Notice of Default period.

The most typical Chapter to file to stop a foreclosure is a **Chapter 13**, because you can propose a plan of repayment that

catches up on the past due amounts you owe to your mortgage or other lenders against your home, over a 36 to 60 month period.

You can file for bankruptcy on your own or with a lawyer. The first option is cheaper, but some individuals are making errors in the process and not getting approved, then they often have to wait several months before they can reapply.

Hiring a lawyer can help ensure an accurate filing, but charges for filing a bankruptcy can be steep. If you are considering bankruptcy and using a lawyer to file, ask the lawyer what you may expect as the outcome if you file for bankruptcy and then ask the lawyer to put his fees in writing. Depending on your unique situation, a bankruptcy might just end up being a costly delay of the inevitable loss of your home.

What are the Tax Implications of Default and Foreclosure?

Until 2007, homeowners who lost their homes in foreclosure or modified their loans were often shocked to learn that they owed taxes on the home they had lost. In 2007, the federal government passed the *Mortgage Forgiveness Debt Relief Act of 2007 which generally allows taxpayers to exclude income from the discharge of debt on their principal residence. Debt reduced through mortgage restructuring, as well as mortgage debt forgiven in connection with a foreclosure, qualifies for this relief.*

This provision applies to debt forgiven in 2007, 2008 or 2009. Up to $2

million of forgiven debt is eligible for this exclusion ($1 million if married filing separately). The exclusion does not apply if the discharge is due to services performed for the mortgage company or any other reason not directly related to a decline in the home's value or the taxpayer's financial condition.

Keep in mind that the Debt Forgiveness Act of 2007 pertains to federal income taxes only. The State of California has a mortgage debt forgiveness program too, but it differs from the federal law. **Please consult a tax professional for advice on federal or state tax law**.

If you are having difficulty resolving a tax problem (such as one involving an IRS bill, letter or notice) through normal IRS channels, the Taxpayer Advocate Service may be able to help. For more information, you can also call the TAS toll-free case intake line at 1-877-777-4778, TTY/TDD 1-800-829-4059.

In some cases, you may qualify for free or low-cost assistance from a Low Income Taxpayer Clinic (LITC). LITCs are independent organizations that represent low income taxpayers in tax disputes with the IRS. Find information on a LITC in your area at http://www.irs.gov/advocate/content/0,,id=151026,00.html.

Look out for Mortgage Foreclosure Rescue Scams

Foreclosure rescue fraud is sweeping the country and can end up costing you the home you are desperately trying to save from foreclosure.

Some of the fastest growing frauds sweeping the nation are foreclosure rescue scams. These scams involve thieves who steal people's homes and equity after promising to help save their homes from foreclosure.

Public notices of foreclosure proceedings usually trigger mail, phone, and even door-to-door solicitations.

You should steer clear of any company that initiates such contact, demands a fee before providing services, or advises cutting contact with the mortgage company, which can delay legitimate options for preventing foreclosure proceedings.

Foreclosure rescue scams usually fall into one of the following four categories:

1) Phantom help

In this scam, the supposed rescuer charges very high fees for basic phone calls and paperwork that you can easily do yourself without any assistance. Or, the rescuer will make promises to represent you, but will not follow through. This is

really a "too little too late" scam as in the helpless homeowner receives too little (or no) help that is too late to stop the foreclosure from taking place.

2) Bailout

Here the scammer claims to assist you by promising you can stay in the house as a renter and buy the house back once things have been "fixed" if you transfer the title of the house to the scammer. The way the scammers get the house varies, but each method ends with you not being able to buy the house back and the supposed rescuers get most, if not all, of the equity.

3) Bait and switch

The bait and switch with foreclosure scams involves signing away the ownership of your home. The scammers will tell you that they are signing documents for a new loan that will solve your problems. In reality, you may be signing **forged documents** that will give the crooks ownership of your home. To make matters worse, you will still be liable for the mortgage even though you no longer own the home.

4) Bankruptcy Foreclosure

The scammer may promise to negotiate with your mortgage company or to get refinancing on your behalf **if you pay a fee up front**. Instead of contacting your mortgage company or refinancing your loan, the scammer instead pockets the fee and files a bankruptcy case in your name, and sometimes without your knowledge. A bankruptcy filing often stops a home foreclosure, but only temporarily. The bankruptcy process is also complicated, expensive and unforgiving. For example, if you fail to attend your first meeting with the creditors, the bankruptcy judge will dismiss the case and the foreclosure will continue. If this happens, you could lose the money you paid to the scammer and *still* lose your home on top of it. Too make matters worse, a bankruptcy stays on your credit report for ten years and can make it very difficult to get a job, get life insurance, buy a car, rent an apartment or buy a home.

Red Flags – If you're looking for someone to help prevent a foreclosure, be sure to avoid any businesses that…

> *Guarantees* to stop the foreclosure process, no matter what your circumstances.
>
> Tells you not to contact your mortgage company, lawyer or credit or housing counselor.
>
> Collects a fee before providing you with any services.
>
> Accepts payment only by cashier's check or wire transfer.
>
> Encourages you to lease your home so you can buy it back over time.
>
> Tells you to make your mortgage payments directly to them instead of your mortgage company.

Tells you to transfer your property deed or title to them.

Offers to buy your house for cash at a fixed price that is not set by the housing market.

Offers to fill out paperwork for you.

Pressures you to sign paperwork you have not had a chance to read or that you do not understand.

Foreclosure is difficult enough without scams being involved in the process. Follow these do's and don'ts.

Do not bury your head in the sand. The problem will not go away, and will only get worse if you ignore it.

Do make sure that you are in foreclosure. If you are behind in payments, you will receive what is called a **deficiency notice**. These letters notify you of your delinquency and give you a chance to resolve the debt. If you receive a Notice of Trustee's Sale, or similar document, you are in foreclosure.

Do speak with your mortgage company. Try to work with your mortgage company to restructure the payments or refinance the loan.

Do learn the laws regarding foreclosure for your state. It is important to know how much time you have to resolve the issue.

Do contact a counseling agency. This is often too big of an issue for a person to handle on his or her own. Make sure that the counselor is

certified by the Department of Housing and Urban Development (HUD). Their website is www.hud.gov.

Be careful when choosing a counselor and pay attention to the certification requirement recommended above. **You should not have to pay for legitimate housing counseling.**

Do contact an attorney. You can find one through the National Association of Consumer Advocates (www.naca.net) or by contacting your local Bar Association. Homeowners in the Bay Area can contact *www.sfbar.org/lawyerreferrals/index.aspx or call Community Legal Services in East Palo Alto at (650) 326-6440. Assistance is also available in Spanish.*

Do not sign a contract under duress. Always request to take time to review any documents on your own and at your own pace. Do not sign a document that you do not understand.

Do not enter into oral agreements. Get in any offers in **writing** and tell whoever is making the offer that you and/or your representative will review any and all offers.

Do not make payments to any party other than your mortgage company.

Do not sign a home-sale contract where you are not released from your existing mortgage.

Do not sign a quit claim deed without being specifically instructed by your attorney or representative to do so. Do not agree to any deal that allows you to rent the property and then buy it back at a later date.

Do not accept an offer from somebody who wants to make good on your missed payments and take the house off your hands in exchange for documents that assign them the surplus from the foreclosure sale. Think

about it, if you owe $200,000 on your mortgage, plus arrears of $10,000, and your house is worth $250,000, you stand to make money on a sale.

Frequently Asked Questions

Q: What happens after I miss a loan payment?

Generally, the first thing a mortgage company will do is telephone you or write to offer you help. They may telephone or write and demand that you pay the loan arrears and penalties. Keep in mind that these calls and letters are designed to collect money for loan payments and the mortgage company or his agent will use collection tactics. STAY CALM. If you are limited English proficient, ask for an agent that speaks your language. The Fair Debt Collection Practices Act imposes rules on debt collectors; they may only telephone you between the hours of 8 a.m. and 9 p.m. local time, the caller may not make repeated calls to annoy you and may not use profane language or threaten you. If you want to stop the calls, you may write to the mortgage company and invoke your right to get notices only in writing. If you think the caller has violated these rule, consult a lawyer.

Q: Am I exposed to a Deficiency Judgment on my mortgage after foreclosure of the first mortgage?

As noted above, California allows a mortgage company to choose to proceed with a judicial or non-judicial foreclosure. If the mortgage company uses non-judicial foreclosure (does not take you to court) the mortgage company gives up the right to collect any additional money from the homeowner even if the money obtained in the foreclosure sale does not cover the full amount of the underlying loan.

In a Judicial foreclosure the mortgage company takes the homeowner to court and can get the property and a money judgment up to the full amount of the debt plus costs.

Q: Am I exposed to a deficiency Judgment after foreclosure on the second mortgage?

If the second or junior mortgage is a "purchase money" mortgage (one that you got to purchase the property originally) the second mortgage is extinguished. ALL purchase money mortgages, whether first or second loans, are extinguished in a foreclosure.

If you have refinanced your home after the original purchase mortgage and have a second or junior mortgage, the mortgage company on the second mortgage can go to court and seek a judgment for the amount of the second mortgage. This means that if you have a junior or second mortgage and go through foreclosure of the first mortgage, you may still be liable for the full amount of the junior mortgage.

Q: What is my exposure to taxation if I reform my loan or go through foreclosure?

Because tax issues are complicated and vary so much depending on the *circumstances, it is best to **seek guidance from a tax professional**. The Debt Forgiveness Act of 2007 does provide some relief to taxpayers in foreclosure. Please keep in mind that while the federal Internal Revenue Service has provided tax relief to homeowners in foreclosure, the State of California has not done so at the time this Guide was printed. You may be liable to the State of California for income taxes..*

If you owe property taxes on your home and the property is foreclosed. You do not have to pay the property tax.

Q: Can I go to jail for failing to pay my mortgage?

NO! But, in some circumstances described in this Guide, the lender or someone whom the lender has given the claim to may get a judgment against you and collect money by attaching property or bank accounts in your name and may garnish or attach your wages, collecting a percentage of your wages for each pay period.

Q: Will a default, short sale, or foreclosure damage my credit and if so, to what extent?

Yes. All of these will severely damage your credit but, the damage can be mitigated and you can rebuild your credit. It is hard to do this on your own and free assistance is available through Consumer Credit Counselors of California. If you are experiencing money troubles, call 800.777.7526 or email info@cccssf.org.

Q: After my house has been sold in foreclosure, how much time do I have to move?

This question is difficult to answer because there are many variables. However, a new owner cannot force you to move out by threatening you or telling you to leave the property. The new owner must go to court and seek a judgment of possession

– that means the Court, in a written document, must say that you have to move out. If you get any papers telling you to move, don't panic. In most cases you will have six weeks or more to move out. Tenants in properties that have been foreclosed have special rights and should consult a lawyer if they are asked to move or served with legal papers.

Q: Whom should I contact if I think I've been taken advantage of by a foreclosure rescue scammer?

Contact a housing counselor
Contact a private attorney or your local Legal Aid office (See information on Page 1)
Contact your local Better Business Bureau
Contact the Federal Trade Commission at 1-877-FTC-HELP

Compiled by:		Provided by:
UNIVERSITY OF SAN FRANCISCO,		COMMUNITY LEGAL SERVICES IN E. PALO ALTO
SCHOOL OF LAW		2117 (B) UNIVERSITY AVENUE
2130 FULTON STREET		EAST PALO ALTO, CA 94303
SAN FRANCISCO, CA 94117		TEL: (650) 326-6440

With the generous assistance of Fenwick and West, LLC.
February, 2009

Make questions learn and research be more open to check simple pages from people they can may help you and or give you a pointer how to do it and most of all for people can really give you the correct information about the problem you face and do everything together as a couple [if you married]
or even if your single keep the information in all the documents and answer all the questions and phone calls the lender do to you never hang up the phone never answer bad words or even explain about your life.

i did few research and i learn every single time to check websites can help us with questions and correct answers

http://network.hispanicpro.com/profiles/blogs/learn-more-about-discussion-panelists-of-professionals-in-banking?xg_source=msg_mes_network

few people going to give the real answer most of them not.

as California survey result was 60% of people living here we paid more taxes for more of the items we been need around our lives so why let Title plus to come to work without license and the proper documentation to do mortgages contracts?

these is one of many surveys and answers California need to reach out and have more careful about it

http://www.breitbart.com/Breitbart-California/2014/04/13/Record-High-60-of-Californians-Say-They-Pay-Too-Much-Tax

Ahead of the April 15 tax deadline, a record-high 60% of Californians say that they pay "much more" or "somewhat more" in taxes than they should, according to a recent survey by the Public Policy Institute of California (PPIC) (and noted by John Seiler of Calwatchdog.org and Stephen Frank ofCApoliticalnews.com).

However, as PPIC Mark Baldassare notes at Fox & Hounds, Californians still believe that the answer is to tax wealthy earners or corporations more--not to reform and broaden the current tax system.

The PPIC survey, which was conducted in March among 1,702 adults, notes:

> While about half of Californians view the state and local tax system as fair, a record-high 60 percent of adults say they pay much more (30%) or somewhat more (30%) than they feel they should in state and local taxes; 35 percent think they pay about the right amount and 3 percent say they pay less than they should. Opinions of likely voters are similar.

However, as Baldassare notes, that view of the tax system remains tied to a view that the wealthy do not pay enough, and that the state should restore and extend funding for services. That makes the prospects for fiscal reform rather dim: "If tax reform proponents ask voters to raise taxes or to make changes to the state and local tax system any time soon, they will need to be mindful of voters' current views on these issues," he writes.

Other findings in the survey include increasing concern about water, which is named as the state's second-most important issue after jobs and the economy; a record-high level of support for immigrants, with 65% saying that they are a benefit to the state; and near record-low levels of support for President Barack Obama, albeit still just above 50%.

The state also remains staunchly liberal on a variety of social issues, from abortion to gun control.

So my own thoughts are mortgages services and even Ginnie Mae why they are free to do whatever they want and never check them the mess of homes inside one CD and companies as Ginnie Mae, CHase, Wells Fargo and other banks are complete agree these "clerical mistakes" or negligence come to their favors and more people decide to move out their homes

i can said 99.9 % of those homes may have another "attack" house in their names and nobody said nothing in our case the Assessor office of Sacramento was complete blind and let it go..profits? i betcha Assessor office of Sacramento receive few of them .

i call different Assessor offices in different counties as Ventura, KIngs, Orange even our own here at Kern County and every one said the same answer

"if the mistake is done inside these office 2 weeks tops for the information of the real homeowner name be in the correct home , if Title company do that not more or top of 2 months but in our case was almost 3 years and everyone Assessor Office of Sacramento, Title Plus and GMFS even Ginnie Mae was complete quiet and ignored the consequences these can be done to us.

we send plenty faxes, emails, phone calls to Washington, Sacramento and Louisiana for that time be enough to paid our mortgage and even few of our student loans .

a friend at facebook once said to me

" The big tax paying companies are fleeing the State because of over-regulation,"

is true!!!!

and the sad part most of those companies take away jobs for families who need to support children, home and bills.

i believe doing these book for me is the way to express our experience to people have more careful when they sign a document comes in you name and you dream home and i take the bases as Cesar Chavez help people working in fields to have rights to have water and restrooms few people believe he was a marxist ideas...really bring water and restrooms to the fields and place to keep 30 minutes break under a umbrella and other 2 15 minutes to eat...

Back to the houses look over MERS

to found out who is your lender, who is your servicer and who is you guarantor and main investors and is where you can learn about all in your mortgages documentation.

contact

FHA

CFBB

California State Board of Equalization

make research and found where you live…

be as us 1% of the 99.99% resist to lost their property for clerical mistakes or negligence

check your credit is places for free as

hhttp;//www.creditkarma.com

in our case we receive different offers from the lenders

1. we can not qualify for FHA but is much better program can help us…

careful not other program can be better or protect you more as FHA does and as well these can be as well balloon payment.

2. Balloon payment

worst of all your start with one amount said $590 for few months and after [6 months] goes to $1290 and or maybe in [4 months] $2900 or more so be far away from these program.

3. request of occupied conveyance means you care for the house until the "short sale" is done   but not rights for you in all.

is also a program name KEEP YOUR HOME CALIFORNIA

other States may have it too so is good to do research

Helpful Links

A wide array of free services and information is available through these organizations:

- Making Home Affordable
- Avoiding Foreclosure - US Department of Housing and Urban Development (HUD)
- Mortgage Facts for Consumers - Federal Trade Commission
- Stop Mortgage Fraud - California Office of the Attorney General
- Mortgage Modification and Foreclosure Scams Alert - Department of Corporations and Department of Real Estate
- Consumer Alert - Department of Real Estate (DRE)
- Mortgage Forgiveness Debt Relief Act and Debt Cancellation
- Homeownership Preservation Foundation
- Know Your Options
- Fannie Mae Foreclosure Help
- Freddie Mac Avoiding Foreclosure Resource Center
- Trouble Making Payments - Veterans Affairs
- Military One Source - for service members who are having financial difficulties with their mortgages
- Approved Credit Counseling Agencies - US Department of Justice
- Financial Literacy - Department of Financial Institutions (D
-
- Employment Development Department (EDD)
- Foreclosure Help Santa Clara County

phone # 888 954 5337

always need to ask and make questions for any little thing you may don't understand as well is always good to do questions.

Mortgage companies are not your friends nor banks, not lenders, or title companies not even closers all of them are a community of people ready to found a solution how to destroy you if you are not in their level of income for them to earn money from you and your credit, in real life they are as the wolf in little red riding hood tale these real estate community is ready to destroy families livelihood and careers and add more people at homeless centers but as well these real estate community knows and finally wake up without the basis for a nation all going to be remove and the basis of a nation is a family without them is not communities/neighbourhoods , and schools, not towns and equally in these not taxes for the Government and what happens?

was a complete weak up for the Government to have programs as make you home affordable or keep your home California as many other States, but not take it so easy not everything is happiness or darkness everything has a price and may of that we as a homeowners we been learning to know that.

is a closed of documentation has a title company and insurance and the Assessor office in any State no rest and be honest that mistake need to be removed

1. if that mistake was inside the Assessor office not more of 2 weeks

2, if that mistake was Title company not more of 2 months

because in our case was for almost 3 years and after we open a identity theft police report was like a bomb everyone start to removed our names and legal address from records book and from the consolidation utilities in Sacramento county … the fun part we live in Kern County towns separate 2 hours driving almost 3 and around 200 miles one from the other.

contact with your congressman or congresswoman ask for help and make a solution if the manner with Assessor's offices or federal documentation

contact with your district representative you paid taxes and for the basis for help

as well as places as Central California legal Assistance

559 570 1200

 or California Rural Legal Assistance

415 777 2755

not give up if they said "we can not help you" that is the main answer from a government worker can not do nothing but can take a paid check.

Ginnie Mae was one of the investors in our home they look as CD we been contact with them since 2011 , 2012 and 2013 not answer in all even 2014 , but please dont do nothing against the government office because in that case, you end even arrest warrant and judge in less of 1 month.

Leslie Maux and Cedric knew of these situation and both as well was explain us Ginnie Mae attorneys going to contact with us… that never happens

today was sad for me April 21/2014 i found a comment from a friend and her home was sad

"

Well we went to the old house yesterday before heading to Mom's for Easter dinner, just to see what is going on with it, as we keep getting calls from the city that it will be condemned soon...it was sad...I finally feel no connection after two years to the place but am still saddened by how the banks have not kept it up...they kicked us out...yet the signs said it was abandoned...would never have left would they have worked with us...got a letter in the mail the mortgage was sold yet again to another company...hopefully they will be able to get it back up to it's old beauty and sell it to someone...we are no longer responsible as it was filed with our bankruptcy...yet they still keep trying to get us to pay for something they made us leave....sooo...soooo sad...we missed the old place, but now even if they offered it to us for a better deal/mortgage payment it's too far gone to be fixed on our income…"

was sad to read her comment and one friend answer her

" You need to make complaints, to HUD & the housing secretary as the bullshit with the banks was to be stopped. They got $284 billion dollars, all of the HUD insurance on foreclosures, got to keep many of the houses. They settle out of court for a few billion dollars and was supposed to change their procedure to help anyone that needed help if you're not getting help start to complain now!!! If you didn't get in on the settlement you can still sue the mortgage companies that did not follow the Secretary of housings letters, from 2009 to 2011 everyone that received settlement money can still sue also. Mortgage companies are not following the rules and you deserve to be compensated"

the point is everyone give message of hope but as a homeowner fighting for your home is difficult sometimes to everything be easy because is not law 100% protect the homeowner not even after the effect these can cause to the economy and everyone ignored the fact these happens under the "blindness eyes of justice"

and more sad to see homeowners losing hope the suppose to be in a country we send soldiers to give peace and democracy to others

"We can't, included the house in our bankruptcy due to their harassment and not working with us….now they've sold it again went from Flagstad to roundpoint and since they couldn't get us due to the bankruptcy they've turned around and sold it again… All this with OUR name still on the mortgage! So it is taking even longer to get our name off the mortgage papers….already has been three years since the process began…and we haven't lived in the house for two years now…all because they wouldn't work with us..our house when we got it was 95,000.00 and that was the value…but the housing bubble happened and even with additions to the home the value dropped to 65,000.00 for the property and house…we had FHA 30 yr fixed…hubby a veteran and still no aid…he lost his 60,000.00+ a year job and our income with both of us was then below 20,000.00 a year with a 750.00 a month house payment and through it all we kept in contact with them trying to keep it and only fell behind d twice but caught up then got 2 months behind due to other bills we afforded during the 60,000.00 a year income time frame… When they harass you by coming to your home and work you have no choice but to file bankruptcy like we had to…only thing that stopped them, but now we are still dealing with this B.S.!!!..The kicker? The house is in our names still, yet they removed items off the property that belonged to us and have changed the locks but still they say its ours and we can pay on it to get it back?..wtf….they let the basement flood and mold is bad inside and it ruined the furnace and water heater which were in basement…. Even if they wanted to work it out now we couldn't afford to take it back… That's the irony!!!!…And I wrote HUD in detail in regards to all this, sent three emails and got no reply to any of it…our bankruptcy lawyer says to ignore all mail/calls/letters/emails as they cannot do anything to us but keep it in our name til it sells…usually up to three years…but could take 7!!! They aren't trying to clean it up and market it to sell though…. Bunch of bull…

people is losing faith in each of the people they have as their representatives today i call to the office of our congressman David Valadao still can not contact with him or his representative Alicia Wolfe and the worst thing is JUne is coming up and elections as well..

same species vote for me we can help!!!

promise listen to you!!!

if you give me your vote we can remove and help you out your troubles!!!

all lies...

emails are with offers many homeowners fail to receive and ends to be a perfect scam make homeowners give their home keys for less of $2000

never fail check and destroy these type of information can affect instead of help

"

Borrower: Maria Garza   *Call Toll-free:* (888) 832-6794

Property Location: Shafter CA

Lender: ON FILE

Status: ELIGIBLE DUE TO NEW UNDERWRITING GUIDELINES

Please provide the **Instant Tracking Pin** when Calling: **009936275**

Dear Maria Garza,

Please contact us within (2) business days of receipt of this email by calling
Toll-free 1-888-832-6794 to speak with your assigned housing counselor.

You have been assigned to the Fannie Mae*/FreddieMac*Loss Mitigation Department due to the fact that you have applied in the past for assistance but may have had trouble getting approved. New guidelines effective **February 1st, 2013** permit a new evaluation of your Financial Hardship; with the goal of providing you with Mortgage Relief; restructuring your mortgage payments and interest rate to a level you can afford. Your urgent action is required on this matter; call us today.

Call us at 1-888-832-6794 to speak with your assigned housing counselor today.
Even if you have been previously denied you may be eligible NOW!

Based on current guidelines, you pre-qualify for assistance with your mortgage.
*Qualified Applicants May Save up to 65% or more in Monthly Payment Savings
*Foreclosures are Cancelled; your Home Loan is brought back **"CURRENT"**
*Interest Rates reduced as low as 2%; homeowners are reporting *RELIEF*
**Guaranteed Results through our program - call for details*

Due to the number of requests being made for assistance, please contact us within (2) business days of receipt of this email and provide the **Instant Tracking Pin** listed below for account verification purposes:

Instant Tracking Pin: 009936275

Sincerely,

FannieMae*/FreddieMac*Loss Mitigation Department

Eligibility Division

1-888-832-6794

---

all these type of email are complete scams never answer in all.

so we watch in the news about a company Cole & Crisp make a fraud against thousand of homeowners around Kern County elevated the prices of the homes and resaled them in low prices with friends and family members so as we was explain but Attorney General Mr Gordon our case was more about Federal level we contact with these Superior Court located at Fresno and i receive these answer

hank you for your e-mail Maria

The Court's Alternative Dispute Resolution program can refer a mediator to assist you only if the other side is willing to do so as well. If there is no lawsuit filed the mediation would be <u>voluntary for both sides</u>. If a civil lawsuit was filed in our court and if the venue was in our jurisdiction, only then would the mediation be MANDATORY and the jurisdiction would depend on what county the contract was agreed to or signed.

If the jurisdiction was not in Fresno County or let's say for example, it was in Sacramento

then you could utilize that county's court's Self-Help Center for information or you can contact the Calif. Legal Services Sacramento office for assistance. Here is their link:

http://lawhelpca.org/organization/legal-services-of-northern-california-sacrame?ref=GWJa4

Fresno's office is: http://www.centralcallegal.org/.

well i contact with Sacramento and they explain me was impossible to help us because he give me a sample is like a relative of us do a crime i don't going to be able to go to court against them in the same way his hands was closed for him literally for help to our case

so i ask if what happens to us was legal and he said NO!!! but still he can not do nothing against Sacramento County because his office was as minor brother for these office..

so our rights?

lawhelpca.org/organization/legalservices /Sacramento big brother Assesor office of Sacramento was untochable?

we receive another email and contact again to another ADS

point is people get frustrated and stop..and walk out of their homes in our case we tried to don't.

If resources are informing you that your case is a federal matter you may contact the number below

for assistance. It is the Eastern District of California - U.S. Courts telephone number. They may be able to assist you. They also have an ADR program

CM/ECF Helpdesk

Phone: (866) 884-5525 & (866) 884-5444

E-Mail: caed_cmecf_helpdesk@caed.uscourts.gov

The clerk's number: Clerk's Office Main Number 559-499-5600 - See more at: http://www.caed.uscourts.gov/caednew/index.cfm/judges/contacts/fresno-contact/#sthash.8x8_Rc.dpof

From: Maria Garza [mailto:mariagarzasea@gmail.com]

still waiting for answer.

meantime we found another attorney from a friend at facebook and everything i said to her was not true all about our names be included in another home in different county was impossible

i hang up…

another attorney call and looks he knows more about it and we send documents i been "fishing around?"

maybe but we have to fix these situation

today we learn new and wonderful tool your Small claim office inside the Superior Courthouse, yes !!!!!!

finally light come out and we have rights you can go and ask for help and justice is not too blind after all and even the people inside that office for once are humans, yes those type of people you can ask questions and nice answer back to you, those people check your papers and explain how to do yourself and check with a phone call where to send you claim, Finally was done was complete as rainbow really exist and found it

as well we learn from a friend

Dear Maria,

Ever heard the term "conventional financing" and wonder what that means?

Basically, the money you borrow to finance your home likely comes from a huge pool of funds that ultimately comes from investors. The system works like this: a local lender has $10 million and makes 100 mortgages, each for $100,000. Having loaned out all that cash, you would think that the lender would now be out of business, but that's not the case. The lender now owns 100 mortgages, which are assets that can be sold.

The lender sells the mortgages to organizations such as Fannie Mae and Freddie Mac. Once the loans are sold, then the lender has more cash to make more loans.

Here's the catch: Fannie Mae and Freddie Mac don't buy every loan. They only by loans that meet certain rules and criteria, and these loans are called conventional loans.

For more information on loan programs, please give me a call. I can help you discover the right options for you.

Best regards,

RECORDING REQUESTED BY
AND WHEN RECORDED MAIL TO
NAME: TitlePid, LLC
ADDRESS: 7368 Florida Blvd, Ste 100B
CITY: Baton Rouge
STATE/ZIP: LA 70806
MAIL TAX STATEMENTS TO
NAME: Ramon D. Bana and Idalia F. Bana
ADDRESS: 337 Clorinde St
CITY: Vallejo
STATE/ZIP: CA 95963
Title (order No, Escrow or Loan No.) A-20140706181
SPACE ABOVE THIS LINE FOR RECORDERS USE

GRANT DEED

The undersigned grantor(s) declare(s) that the documentary transfer tax is $0.00 NAME CHANGE TRANSFER and is

__computed on the full value of the interest or property conveyed, or is

__computed on the full value less the value of liens or encumbrances remaining thereon at the time of sale,

__Unincorporated area: _X__City of Sacramento, and

FOR A VALUABLE CONSIDERATION, receipt of which is hereby acknowledged, RAY VALLES, III AND MALINDA VALLES

hereby REMISE(S), RELEASE(S) AND FOREVER QUITCLAIM(S) to RAYMUNDO VALLES, III AND MALINDA VALLES

the following described real property in the City of Sacramento, County of Sacramento, State of California:

LOT 73, as shown on the "Plat of Scottsfield" recorded in Book 190 of Maps, in the official records of said County

Dated: August 24, 2011

RAY VALLES, III

Malinda Valles
MALINDA VALLES

as you can see our names was add in a home we never buy , rent or live in all in a book of a county as Sacramento .

Sacramento is a town and county to the Norht of us 300 miles and around 4 hours very diffeent town as Kern County is...

and we call to these Assesor office and ask for why our names was involved in these home we ask the title company why our names was add in these home for an affidavit sign with our names on it and nothing

was like tried to speak with a small 2 years.

GMFS

Your Lender for Life

Robin Hogan
GMFS, LLC
7389 Florida Blvd., Suite 200A
Baton Rouge, LA 70806
NMLS ID # 351767, Branch ID
Company NMLS #64997

Inside: Open Immediately

Personal Loan Review for

we call with her we ask several times for our names was removed from that home

since Nov 28 2011 and never was removed in all all way to 2013 until she decide to said to us to contact with her attorney

and her attorney was believing was a blessing for us to be add to a program help us to do the mortgage of the house.

we qualify for the hope for homeonwers yes!!!!

that is a Federal program by the President Barack Obama yes !!!

but not we was not "blessing for the clerical mistake "

we was involved in all

that was not blessing in all.

my dream was to become a pharmacist technician have a job and paid my bills

as everyone else

not to be in these hell of documents where lenders or servicers used our names without our authorizations and add them in other counties and homes we never belong to us

and that means we need to accept the consecuences of their mistakes and be

with life as nothing happens in all

we have names in our credit from credit cards we never open

we have 3 children and we end with 2 more almost our ages and because their names are hispanic roots as us we suppose to know them

and keep everything in our records without talk or ask to be removed it?

not make sense but is the new type of virus name Title companies and Lenders and banks who said to us these is a blessing be with that and continue your life.

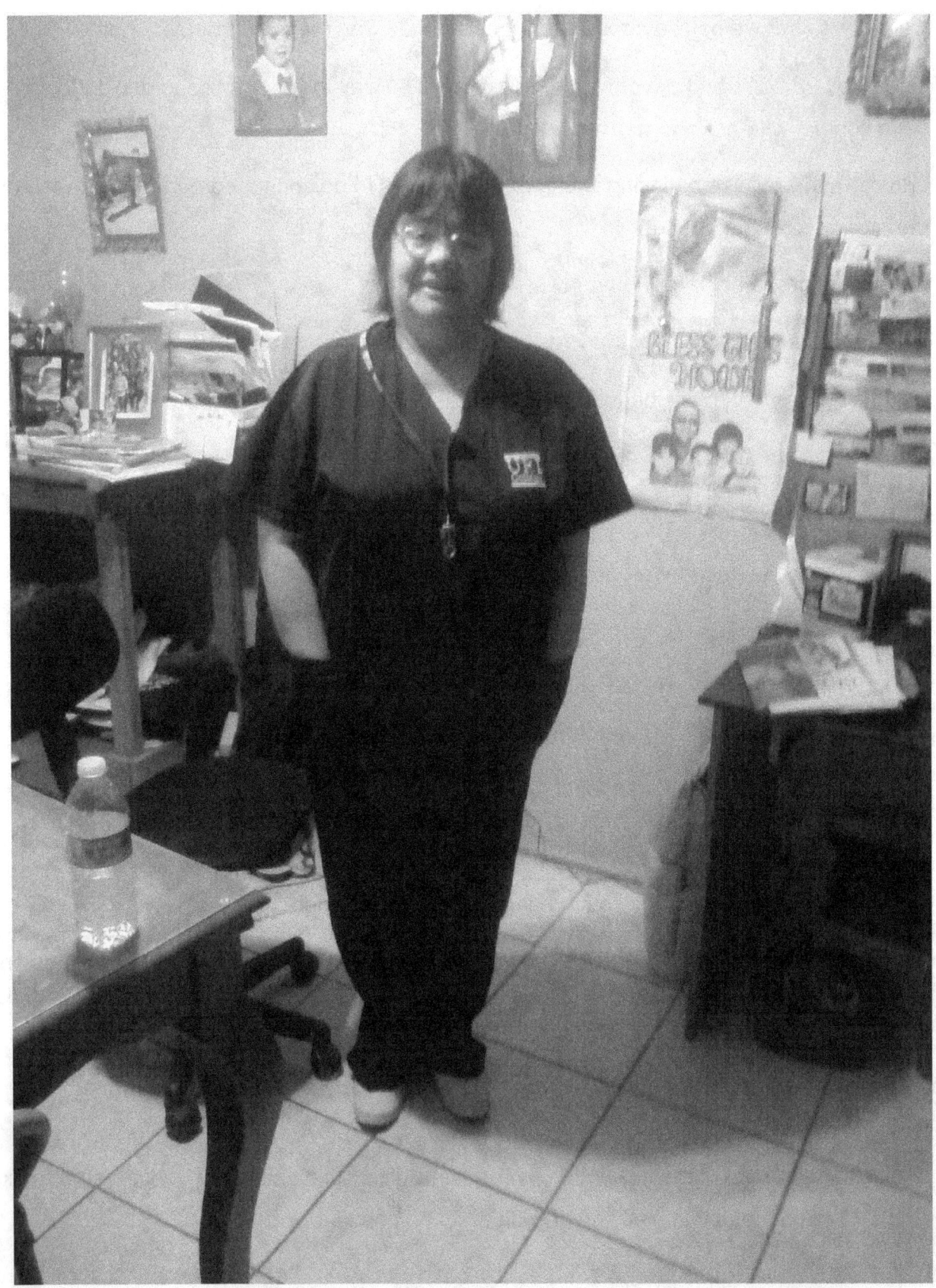

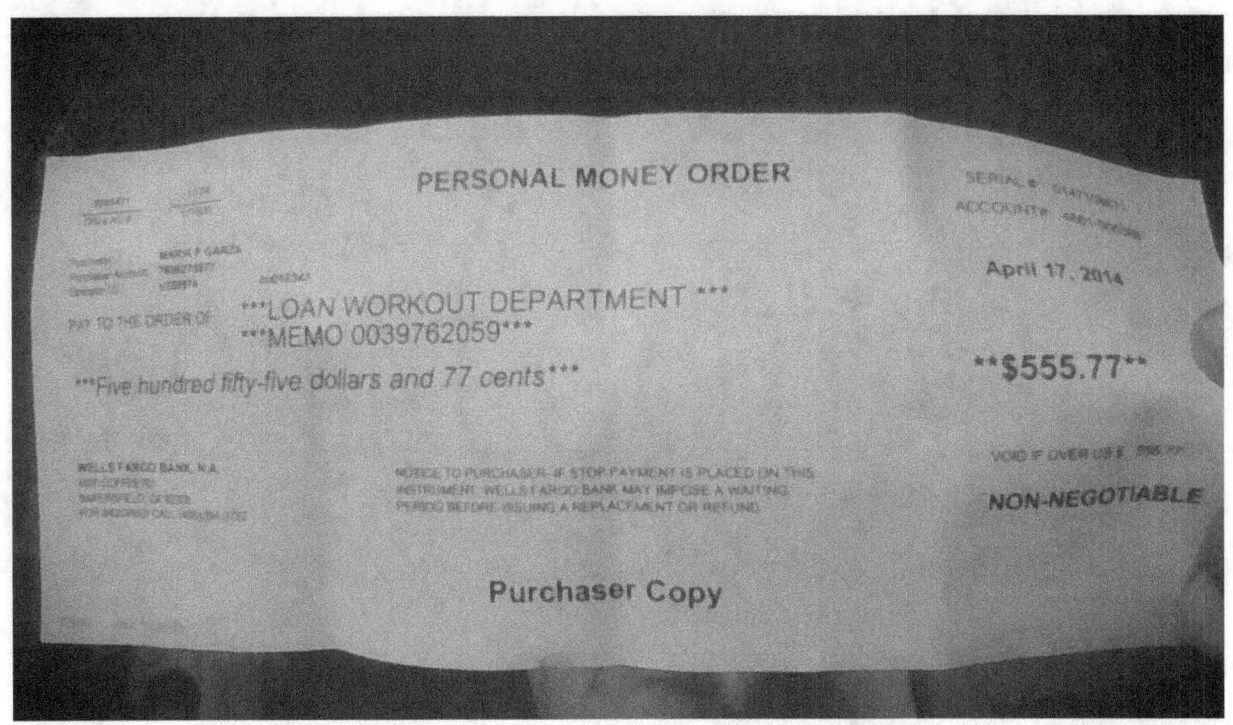

we suppose to be in a trail bases means for 3 months to make these amount of period

RECORDING REQUESTED BY
AND WHEN RECORDED MAIL TO
NAME: TitlePro, LLC
ADDRESS: 7300 Florida Blvd, Ste 1000
CITY: Baton Rouge
STATE/ZIP: LA 70806
MAIL TAX STATEMENTS TO
NAME: Ramon D. Barra and Maria P. Barra
ADDRESS: 857 Clarence St
CITY: Shafter
STATE/ZIP: CA, 93263
Title Order No. Escrow or Loan No.:   A-5061670024

SPACE ABOVE THIS LINE FOR RECORDER'S USE

GRANT DEED

The undersigned grantor(s) declare(s) that the documentary transfer tax is $0.00 NAME CHANGE TRANSFER and is

___ computed on the full value of the interest or property conveyed, or is
___ computed on the full value less the value of liens or encumbrances remaining thereon at the time of sale.

___ Unincorporated area _X_ City of Sacramento, and

FOR A VALUABLE CONSIDERATION, receipt of which is hereby acknowledged, RAY VALLES, III AND MALINDA VALLES

hereby REMISE(S), RELEASE(S) AND FOREVER QUITCLAIM(S) to RAYMUNDO VALLES, III AND MALINDA VALLES
the following described real property in the City of Sacramento, County of Sacramento, State of California:

LOT 71, as shown on the "Plat of Southport" recorded in Book ___ of Maps, Map No. ___ records of said county.

Dated: August 24, 2011

RAY VALLES, III

Malinda Valles
MALINDA VALLES

we going to fix these sittuation?

we dont have idea but these 2014 is the last year for us with these mess

we just give you the heads up

fight for anything you believe is yours and before walk out the house where you live and give the keys back

check your credit and look around if you names was used in another home.

and have faith

GOOD LUCK

Maria Pilar Garza

www.ingramcontent.com/pod-product-compliance
Lightning Source LLC
Chambersburg PA
CBHW08161200526
45167CB00019B/3017